AF484496

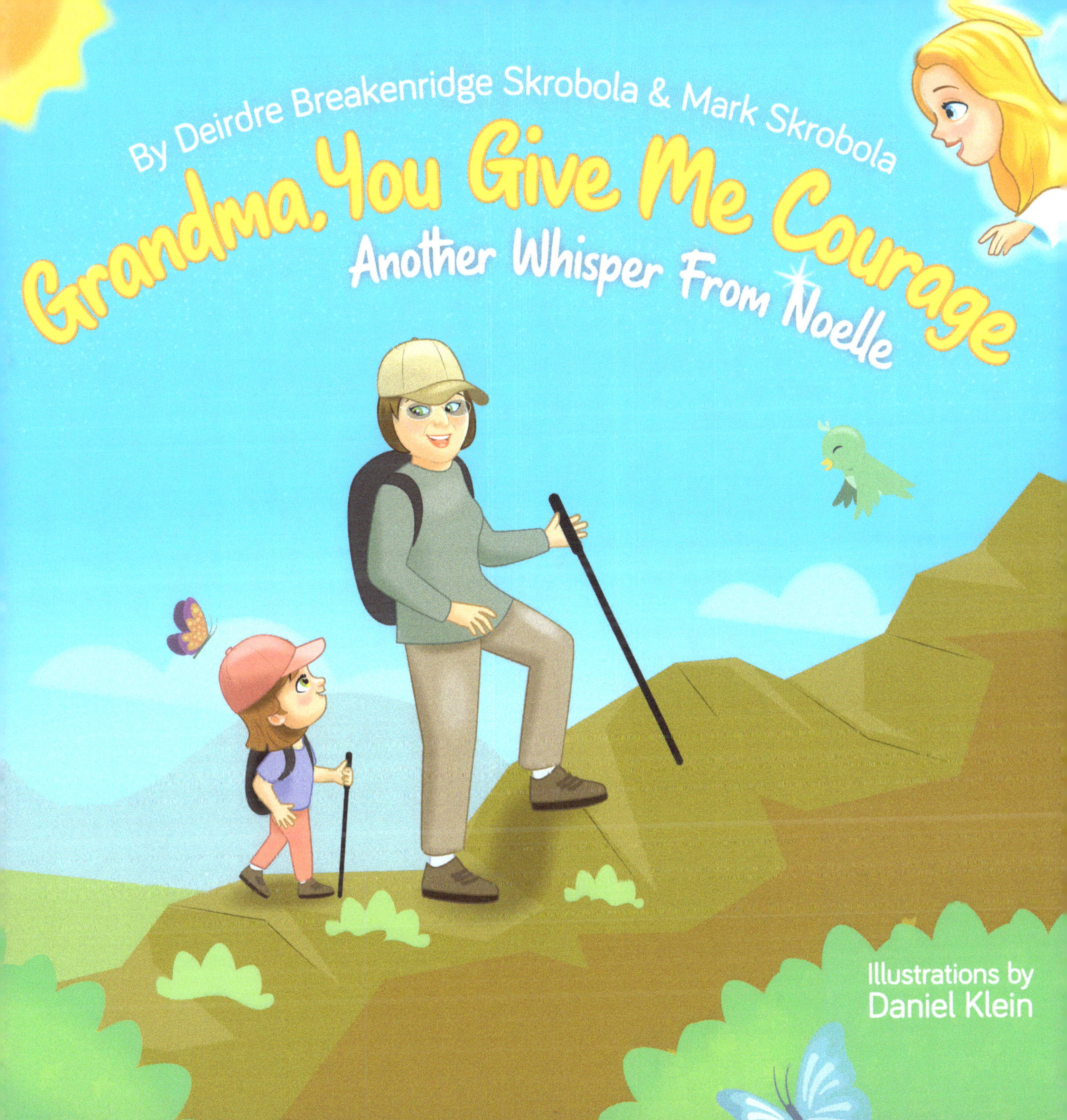

By Deirdre Breakenridge Skrobola & Mark Skrobola
Grandma, You Give Me Courage
Another Whisper From Noelle
Illustrations by
Daniel Klein

This Whisper belongs to

All proceeds go to charity.
Please visit www.awhisperfromnoelle.com/giving for more information.

Grandma, You Give Me Courage
Another Whisper From Noelle
All Rights Reserved.
Copyright © 2023 Deirdre Breakenridge Skrobola and Mark C Skrobola
V1.0

This book may not be reproduced, transmitted, or stored in whole or in part by any means, including graphic, electronic, or mechanical without the express written consent of the authors except in the case of brief quotations embodied in critical articles and reviews.

Paperback ISBN:979-8-218-24135-3
Hardback ISBN: 979-8-218-24257-2

Illustrations by Daniel Klein. All Rights Reserved – Used With Permission.

To our dear and courageous moms,
Carol Skrobola and Edith Ziegler, who
have shown us the true meaning of love
and support. Thank you for your
unwavering courage and for inspiring
us. We dedicate this book to you with
immense gratitude and love.

Ashley-Ann was sitting in her room when she remembered,
"Grandma says there are a lot of adventures to explore."

"I want to stay with my friends and spend time with them,"
sighs Ashley-Ann. "Maybe adventure isn't for me!"

She turned to her friend Lily and said, "Why should I go to the museum, the flower gardens, or the car show?" Ashley-Ann had plenty to talk about with her stuffed animals that day. She wanted a tea party and was not in the mood for adventure.

That night her angel friend, Noelle, visited and whispered in her ear, "Adventure is fun. You get to try new things. How do you know you don't like something if you haven't tried it?"

Ashley-Ann thought about what Noelle shared. She was scared to visit different places and see new faces and was happy with what she already knew.

"I'm not like my grandma. She's brave, and she likes adventure. She went on a real safari with lions, elephants, and giraffes when she was in Africa," thought Ashley-Ann.

Noelle smiled and gently reminded Ashley-Ann, "Your grandma wants to share special moments with you and exciting new ways to learn. With your grandma, you will find the courage and be brave when you explore. You can decide what adventures you like and what you don't like. "

Ashley-Ann's grandma had been on many adventures, from a cruise to Alaska to trips to other far-off places.

Noelle also told Ashley-Ann, "Sometimes you can go on an adventure in your imagination, and grandma will be there leading the way!"

Ashley-Ann loved knowing she could use her imagination to go on an adventure. Because she was curious about a safari, hiking up the tallest mountain, and taking an airplane ride to a beautiful beach.

When Ashley-Ann saw her grandma later that day, she asked, "Grandma, can you tell me some stories about your adventures?" As her grandma shared each experience, Ashley-Ann saw herself with her grandma: Courageous and full of adventure!

Of course, they also took special day trips to the petting zoo, where she could pet real animals. Although Ashley-Ann couldn't touch the dinosaurs or the beautiful stones at the museum, these were adventures she would never forget.

Ashley-Ann ended up loving most of the adventures and learned she could be courageous. Her grandma helped her to explore and to feel brave wherever they went.

Sitting quietly with her grandma, after an adventure to New York City, Ashley-Ann said, "Grandma, I love adventure, but most of all, I love you."

Her grandma hugged her and said, "Ashley-Ann, I love you too. We can always find adventure together."

Grandma gave Ashley-Ann the courage to go on new adventures, and Noelle was right there, every time they explored.

The end

FEEL
F = Face your Fears
E = Have Empathy for Others
E = Live with Ethics and Good Judgment
L = Unleash your Love

The Whisper from Noelle Series

See our other books for sale.

A Whisper from Noelle

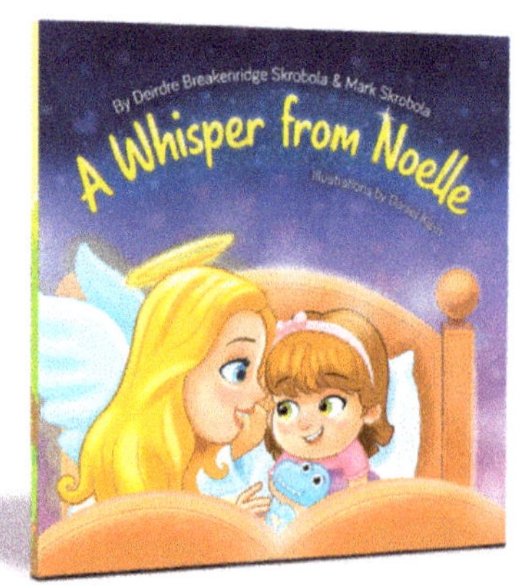

One night, Ashley-Ann receives a very special visit while lying in bed. An angel named Noelle comes to her with a series of loving whispers, each with an important message. As Ashley-Ann shares the angel's whispers with her mommy, readers are given the gift of wisdom that Noelle brings to Ashley-Ann. We learn that knowing how to feel will bring kindness, compassion, courage, and the ability to be true to ourselves. This nurturing, insightful story is sure to be a favorite with readers of all ages.

Grandpa Don't Worry

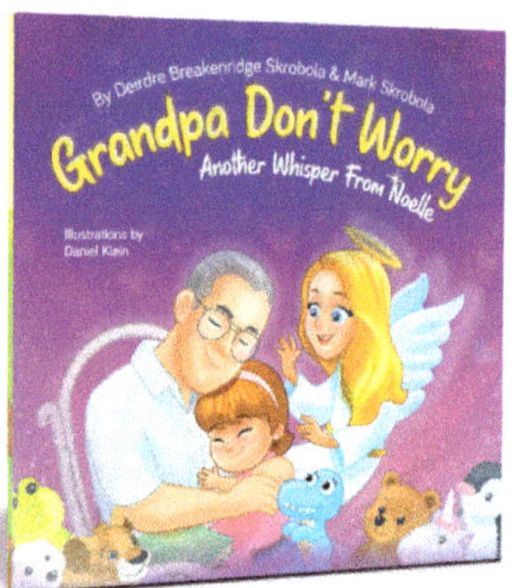

One night, Ashley-Ann receives a very special visit from her friend, an angel named Noelle. In a series of whispers, Ashley-Ann listens closely to hear important messages that she needs to share with her grandpa. Through Noelle, Ashley-Ann discovers that Grandpa has feelings too. He sometimes worries. He wants Ashley-Anne to understand the importance of family values, which include love, strength, caring, and kindness.

Knowing that Ashley-Ann learns about these "Loving Lessons" from Noelle, makes her Grandpa very happy. With these caring messages, children and families can explore feelings and values together and what it means to be kind and to understand each other. This insightful story is sure to be a favorite among readers of all ages.

Daddy Are You Listening

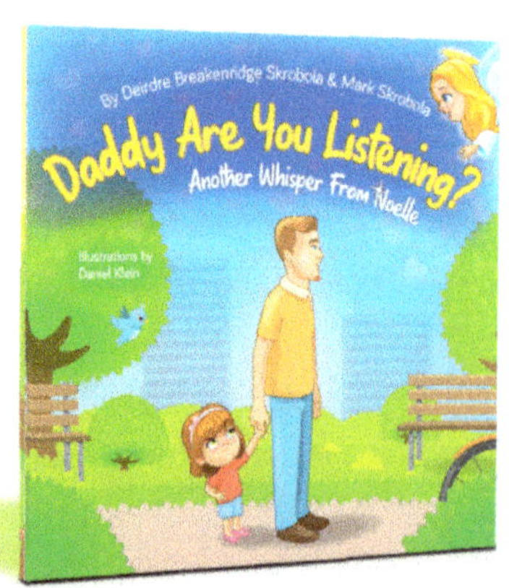

While walking in the park one day, Ashley-Ann is not sure her daddy listens to her. She shares the week's exciting events, and his mind is elsewhere. Ashley-Ann remembers that her friend, Noelle, an angel, recently visited and whispered an important message in her ear. Noelle told Ashley-Ann that her daddy was trying to listen, and she needed to help him. That day in the park, Ashley-Ann learned how to help her daddy be a better listener and what it means to listen to each other. Children and families can explore feelings and values with this caring message. Listening is the first step to caring, kindness, and showing you understand the ones you love. This insightful story will be a favorite among readers of all ages.

Activities

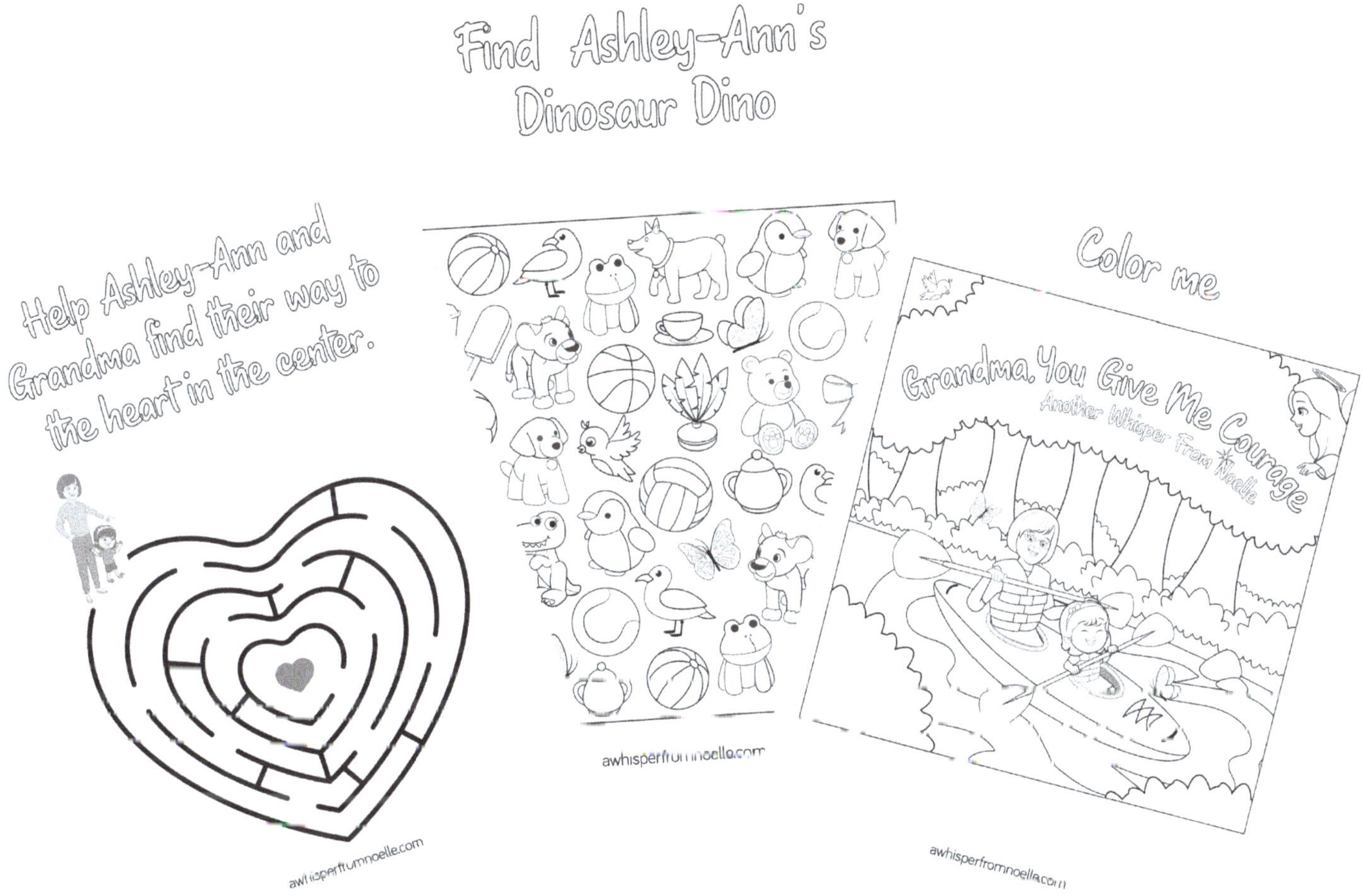
Help Ashley-Ann and Grandma find their way to the heart in the center.
awhisperfromnoelle.com
Find Ashley-Ann's Dinosaur Dino
awhisperfromnoelle.com
Color me
Grandma, You Give Me Courage
Another Whisper From Noelle
awhisperfromnoelle.com

Download our PDF

https://awhisperfromnoelle.com/

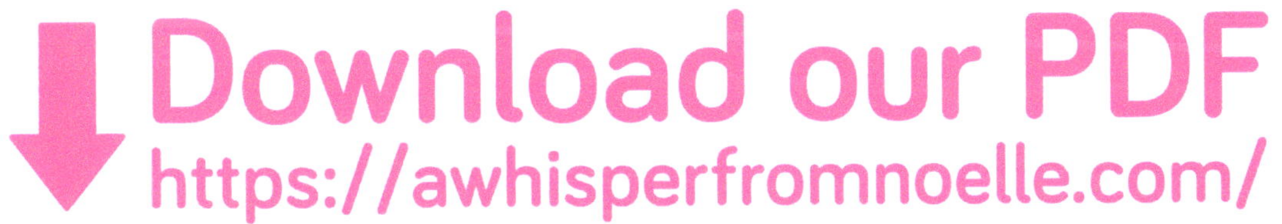

www.ingramcontent.com/pod-product-compliance
Lightning Source LLC
Chambersburg PA
CBHW041816130726
48010CB00004BA/187